THE DEATH OF DEMOCRACY!

Other books by David Hedges

Petty Frogs on the Potomac (1997)
The Wild Bunch (1998)
Brother Joe (2000)
*Steens Mountain Sunrise: Poems
of the Northern Great Basin* (2004)
Selected Sonnets (2006)
*A Funny Thing Happened on My Way
to a Geology Degree* (2011)
*Prospects of Life After Birth:
Memoir in Poetry and Prose* (2019)
The Changer (2021)
*Trump Über Alles: Rhymes
for Trying Times* (2022)
*The Zigzag Papers ~ or ~ Who
Wants Wanda Wasted* (2023)

THE DEATH OF DEMOCRACY!

POEMS BY DAVID HEDGES

ROAD'S END PRESS

The Death of Democracy!
Poetry
David Hedges

Copyright © 2024 David Hedges

FIRST EDITION

All rights reserved. No part of this book may be reproduced in any manner without the express written consent of the author or Road's End Press except for brief excerpts in reviews and articles.

Thanks to the editors of *Poetry, Trinacria, Windfall, Encore,* and *Light: A Journal of Light Verse,* for publishing many of these poems.

"Downwinders" was included in the *Particles on the Wall* traveling exhibit sponsored by Physicians for Social Responsibility.

Road's End Press
326 Pearl Street
Oregon City, Oregon 97045

To order copies, visit roadsendpress.com

Cover art and illustrations by Jim Agpalza
Layout, design, and typography by Andrew Hedges
Proofreading by Valerie Witte

Library of Congress Control Number: 2024906640

ISBN: 978-1-7366102-6-8

Ebook version available.

Printed in the United States of America

I dedicate this book to every American who adheres to the principles of liberty and justice for all and believes we can build a sane society based on equality, community, and human rights.

.

Table of Contents

Preamble

1 - COMBUSTIBLES

The Death Throes of Democracy
O Commandant! My Commandant!
The Predestined Death of Democracy
The Wily Gerrymander
Combustibles
On Stirring the Pot

2 - IN PRAISE OF BILLIONAIRES

Rich People
In Praise of Billionaires
The Trickle-Up Theory
How to Feed the Hungry
Kill the Billionaires
I'm Progressive and I'm Proud

3 - BREAKING WIND

The Hungry Eye
While Politicians Argue Climate Change
The Ghost of Cherry Pond Mountain
Breaking Wind
Oil Futures
Downwinders
The Dillowy Danderhonk
To a Corrupt Politician

4 - TRUMP: "WHAT I LOVE"

Apocalypse Now
CNN Poll
Trump: "What I Love"
Vlad The Impaler
The Ho-Humness of Donald's Misdeeds

Presidential Kiss-Off

5 – TWO BROTHERS WITH BUT ONE REGRET

Alone Among the Creatures
L'État, C'est Trump
Two Brothers With But One Regret

6 – HE LOOKED SO HANDSOME IN HIS UNIFORM

He Looked So Handsome in His Uniform
Ballade for the Gods of War
The War to End All Wars
With Armageddon Just Around the Bend

7 – DAWN OF THE ANTHROPOCENE

I'm Glad My Parents and My Brother Died
The End of the World
Comes the Renaissance
I Dream of Bells
On the Rebirth of America
Dawn of the Anthropocene
Tomorrow

Preamble

In an article in *American Thinker*, author Bryce Buchanan wrote, "The world is heading quite rapidly toward tyranny. We are in a revolutionary period that will dramatically change civilization. Few people understand the gravity of our situation."

He goes on to itemize reasons why people fail to see the light at the end of the tunnel as a freight train barreling toward them.

First is the Normalcy Bias, "a cognitive bias that occurs in times of crisis, leading us to disregard any signs or warnings that we are in danger. . . . a defense mechanism that lulls us into thinking life will just continue as it always has."

Next is the Conformity Bias, where people "look to their social group to tell them what is true. . . . It is the dream of any tyrant to have a population that acquires its beliefs this way. If a political faction can be lied to with impunity, and if blind acceptance of the lies is required to maintain membership in the group, that is a powerful means of control."

He draws on George Orwell's *1984* and Aldous Huxley's *Brave New World* for his third bias. While Orwell predicted the current barrage of fear and coercion, Huxley foresaw "ever more effective methods of mind-manipulation," leading to "a prison without walls . . . a system of slavery where, through consumption and entertainment, the slaves would love their servitude."

Is this our destiny? Living at the whim of an unhinged narcissist, satisfied with our entertainments, our drugs of choice, our iPhone screens, sitting idly by as Big Brother wreaks havoc?

It's been said that when fascism comes to America, it will be wrapped in the flag and carrying a cross. Trump hugs the flag. He waved a Bible in front of a church. In 1935, Sinclair Lewis published *It Can't Happen Here,* a novel in which a fascist dictator rises to power. It *can* happen here. It's unfolding before our eyes.

Is it too late to save the republic? A better question is, if we survive the onslaught of our would-be messiah and his flock, will we have the sense to right the wrongs, the inequalities plaguing our society, that have led us to this tragic point?

David Hedges
Oregon City, Oregon
March 15, 2024

1
COMBUSTIBLES

The Death Throes of Democracy

Sail on, O Ship of State!
Sail on, O Union, strong and great!
Humanity with all its fears,
With all the hopes of future years,
Is hanging breathless on thy fate!

—Henry Wadsworth Longfellow

How in this anxious hour of discontent
Can anyone with open eyes and mind
Be anything but fully cognizant?
Yet roughly half the populace is blind
To evil of the most egregious kind,
That circumvents judicial oversight
And blurs the line dividing wrong from right.

How can democracy survive attacks
On fundamental principles upheld
By courts? Who are these egomaniacs
Whose shady dealings are unparalleled?
And why, when their extremist views are spelled
Out so a simpleton can understand,
Do millions march lockstep behind their band?

The Constitution and the Bill of Rights
Specifically prohibit actions now
Deemed mandatory. Thus the lights
Of liberty are dimmed. Yet those who bow
To autocrats are quick to disavow
Decrees that sanction artifice and fraud
And undermine our prominence abroad.

All those who seek to keep the Ship of State
Afloat see values tumbled overboard.
Left-leaning souls watch hope disintegrate
For peace, the olive branch replaced by sword
And shield, the severance of world accord.
Those on the right rate devastating debt
From reckless borrowing the greater threat.

The overarching answer's not explained
In terms that fit our country's paradigms.
We find a covert rationale ingrained
In politics as practiced in these times
Of bitter partisan debate. High crimes
Committed under propaganda's cloak
Hitch our descendants to oppression's yoke.

O Commandant! My Commandant!
   —with apologies to Walt Whitman

The poop deck on the Ship of State
Is knee deep with the sticky stuff
That pours forth from our Potentate
When he deigns to pontificate
On complex topics off the cuff.

His brain spins like a billiard ball
And ricochets between the beams,
His tweets hold followers in thrall,
His rants scorn law and protocol,
And not a thought means what it seems.

He's hanging by his fingernails.
The quartermaster rings eight bells!
He has an ill wind in his sails
And everything he touches fails,
But on he plunges, through the swells.

He sees his destiny fulfilled!
He'll kill Obamacare, and crown
His head with laurel leaves, and gild
His Oval Office throne, and build
His wall before the ship goes down.

The Predestined Death of Democracy

A republic, if you can keep it.
—Benjamin Franklin, when asked by political activist Elizabeth
Powel if the new nation would be a republic or a monarchy

The founders sealed our fledgling nation's fate
By compromising on a point now giving
Authoritarians the edge: Each state
Shall have two senators. So, voters living
In West Virginia or Wyoming wield
More clout than citizens in Illinois,
New York, or Michigan. The playing field
Tilts hard right. Extremists will destroy
Democracy if they, through cheating, steal
The Senate and the White House. Who can save
Us from dictatorship? The threat is real—
Ben Franklin's turning over in his grave.
The monster clutching at our nation's throat
Fails only if enough good people vote.

The Wily Gerrymander

The Gerrymander, like the Slithy Tove,
Is slightly slimy (think of Karl Rove)
And angular, an ersatz Etch-A-Sketch
Conception rendered by a scurvy wretch
Shape-shifting as he draws a line between
Hard-to-starboard types and those who lean
To port, thus making sure the hoi polloi
Stay in their place—an airtight, ironclad ploy
To maintain order in an otherwise
Untidy world, where Mome Raths jeopardize
The Borogroves, and one-percenters scratch
Their itch for riches with a Bandersnatch.

We're all on tap to burn
In populism's dank and moldy bunker
Where deep down fear and barefaced hatred bunker.

Combustibles

Two sticks are all it takes to start a fire.
Just rub them hard together in the dark
And have dry tinder handy when they spark.
Words may encourage, open eyes enquire,
But only tender touch distills desire—
The exclamation point, the question mark.
Before a circle closes, it's an arc
Where weightlessness attends. There's no place higher.
You see, when everything is round, about
The same horizon everywhere you turn.
The world is flat and everyone's in doubt.
The game has changed. We're all on tap to burn
In populism's dank and moldy bunker
Where deep down fear and barefaced hatred hunker.

On Stirring the Pot

The radiance! A brace of rich
Imaginations running wild
Through daisy fields without a stitch.

And what of you, quixotic child?
Are you a second Joan of Arc,
Or Dor-o-thy, the Meek and Mild?

When running naked, only stark
Will do. Divestiture requires
As much of tinder as of spark.

It's not the weak who fan the fires.
The souls pressed hard against the mold
Know nothing of their own desires.

They wind up winding down as cold
As old refrigerator coils,
Their aspirations pigeonholed.

Until the stuff you're stirring boils,
Nobody knows how hot you've turned,
How plagued with disarray your toils.

Look all about as books are burned.
See how the faces radiate
The sum of what mankind has learned:

We're put on Earth to procreate.
One scratch won't satisfy an itch.
God may be good but greed is great.

2

IN PRAISE OF BILLIONAIRES

Rich People

Rich people haven't got a clue to life.
They either have or are a trophy wife.
Their progeny can't scratch a simple itch
Without proclaiming "Look at me, I'm rich!"
They almost always dress before they dine
And have a sommelier to serve their wine,
A chef to orchestrate their haut cuisine,
A chauffeur for their custom limousine,
An upstairs maid to rectify their mess
And help the lady of the house undress,
A kitchen maid who's fair of shape and face
And doesn't mind succumbing to the chase.
They sit on boards and give to charities,
Oblivious to life's disparities.

*You have to hand it to the billionaires
Or they will send their minions round to take it.*

In Praise of Billionaires

You have to hand it to the billionaires
Or they will send their minions round to take it.
They write the rules: Whatever's yours is theirs,

What's theirs is stashed in offshore banks to make it
Vanish when the taxman comes to call.
The burden falls on you who cannot fake it

With loopholes, credits, and deferrals, all
Designed to guarantee that no one shares
The wealth who's not already made a haul.

The Trickle-up Theory

No matter how you divvy up the pie,
Demand is bound to overtake supply.
There's only so much dough to go around.
This drives us job creators to the ground.

The ninety-nine percent are trying to steal
A bigger slice, and we've begun to feel
The pinch. We're forced to keep our year-old yachts
When next year's models promise sixty knots.

We need our villas in the south of France,
Our island hideaways where we can dance
And play, our Swiss chalets, our Central Park
Apartments, mansions like East Hampton's Arc.

To those who say there's something wrong with greed,
We say, *To each according to his need!*
Our need to feed our offshore bank accounts
In exponential leaps to keep amounts

Ahead of spending has us on the edge.
Instead of jumping off a Wall Street ledge,
We choose to squeeze the poor, the sick, the old,
And turn their abject suffering to gold

With subsidies and tax breaks from our friends
In Congress and the Highest Court, whose ends
Do justify the means, however sordid and perverse
They seem to those who shake their fists and curse.

We billionaires have placed a hammerlock
On all the wealth, but malcontents who squawk
Will praise us to the heavens when we spread
Good will by making sure old folks are fed,

Poor folks have heat in winter, and the ill
Have relatives prepared to foot the bill.
The unemployed will laud us when they learn
The sky's the limit to how much they'd earn

If only they'd been born with ample means
And other measures of their family's genes.
Democracy's passé. Without debate,
We privateers have seized the Ship of State.

How to Feed the Hungry

My plan's to round up billionaires
And lock them tight in feedlot pens
Until they're fat as Frigidaires,
Then do them in like Tyson hens.

Once these elites play out, my plan's
To tackle multimillionaires
And package them in quart-sized cans
To make sure everybody shares.

Their children, born to lives of ease,
Will spare themselves their parents' fate
By paring down necessities
And loving what they thought they'd hate:

A Murphy bed with squeaky springs
Above a Brooklyn butcher shop
And eating out at Burger Kings
And drinking diet soda pop.

Kill the Billionaires

With simple acts of love and kindness.
Shower them with hugs and kisses.
Reward their narcissistic blindness
With reminders of what bliss is.
Turn their beds of roses over.
Feed them bread and water. Fuck it,
Tell them they will roll in clover
Once they up and kick the bucket.
Take away their blue-chip stocks,
Their premium bonds and other shares,
Their duplicate keys to the vault at Fort Knox.
Tell their sotted, snotnosed heirs
To take a flying leap at a rolling
Donut. No more golf. Try bowling.

I'm Progressive and I'm Proud

I'm progressive and I'm proud-proud-proud!
In my thesaurus, Trump's a dirty word,
As loathsome as the bottom of a bird-
Cage, odious as greed. If he's allowed
Free reign, he'll force us begging to our knees
Before his god of wrath. He studies war-
Fare, call himself pro-life, and plays the whore
Behind closed doors. This rat who deals in sleaze,
Who chews the landscape like a chunk of cheese,
Who screws around like fleas and casts the first
Stones in morality debates, is versed
In vice and sly as Mephistopheles.
I'd be the last to vilify his kicks
But I'm a victim of his dirty tricks.

3
BREAKING WIND

The Hungry Eye

The monster hovers like a hungry eye
Where greedy men discharge their industries.
While ozone holes with teeth devour the sky,

Environmental law disciples die
To clear the air where Mephistopheles,
The monster, hovers like a hungry eye.

Polluters feel no pressure to comply—
They call sheep cataracts anomalies.
While ozone holes with teeth devour the sky,

They claim the dermal melanomas lie—
El Niño killed the frogs. (A blind man sees
The monster hover like a hungry eye!)

They focus on a common alibi
To keep goods flowing from their factories
While ozone holes with teeth devour the sky.

The sun becomes a godhead gone awry,
A demon forcing mankind to its knees.
The monster hovers like a hungry eye
While ozone holes with teeth devour the sky.

While Politicians Argue Climate Change

Tree loss doubles in warm era
—Newspaper headline

While politicians argue climate change,
The old-growth giants of the Western slope
Are slowly dying from Earth's warming trend,
A scientific study shows. Kiss firs
And cedars, pines and hemlocks, au revoir.

The West's most stable and resilient stands
Were studied. Ruled out by researchers were
Such local factors as insect attack
And fire suppression. Trees were killed because
The temperature increased by one degree.

The deaths are unexpectedly widespread,
The scientists who wrote the study said.
Their research covered trees of every size
At every elevation, young and old,
From Southwest Canada to Mexico.

According to the study, dying trees
Release their carbon to the atmosphere
While living trees remove it in exchange
For oxygen, which we in turn consume—
A never-ending cycle, until now.

The study doesn't say so, but we've thrown
A monkeywrench into the works, upset
The applecart, by spewing CO_2
With no regard for outcomes such as death
To countless species, possibly our own.

What's worse, we've done so for 200 years!
Some say it's progress, others say it's greed
That's pushed us to the brink. The study fails
To point a finger, or attribute blame.
It focuses on what the numbers mean.

If we believe the study, trees will shrink,
Won't live as long or be as strong. Today,
Sequoia, Sitka spruce, and redwood serve
As "carbon sinks" that capture CO_2,
a greenhouse gas, and keep it tucked away.

We tend to think of stress in human terms.
Trees die of thirst when snowpack fails to stick
Around and melt as summer dries the soil.
We're free (so far) to move about when need
Dictates. Trees can't. The study calls this "stress."

If trees communicate among their own,
And possibly with animals and plants,
As other studies indicate, this means
We are the odd man out (excuse the pun)—
Stumped where Mother Nature is concerned.

This study doesn't talk about the need
To change our ways, give conifers reprieve,
However brief. But others do, and if
We don't take action soon, the trees will fall—
Silently, if no one's there to hear.

The Ghost of Cherry Pond Mountain

Sometimes when Appalachia's valleys brim
With clouds, her mountaintops appear to float
Like islands in a sea of white—a whim
Of nature in a landscape thought remote

Until the dynamiters blew the crowns
Off untold mountains, dumping their debris
Down into streams that furnish towns
With drinking water. Industries are free

To wreak such havoc, federal judges ruled,
Because the White House sabotaged the law
Enacted to protect our streams, and fooled
Us into thinking they had fixed a flaw.

Mountaintop Removal Mining stands
To add one hundred victims to the list
Of mountains it has torn apart. Demands
For coal are great, and companies insist

On turning quicker profits, damn the cost
To people who are poisoned by their need,
The vistas they destroy, the valleys lost
Beneath their avalanche of waste and greed.

The ghost of West Virginia's Cherry Pond
Is seen on misty mornings as a sign
That sea change soon will shift debate beyond
Shareholder dividends—the bottom line—

To what is best for children yet unborn,
The legacy we leave. Defining wealth
With dollar signs has left our nation torn.
It's time we paid attention to our health

And found alternatives to gas and coal.
The sun is up there waiting to be tapped,
The wind, the tides. Let's plug the ozone hole
And tackle global warming. Let's adapt

To less consumption, hold the birth rate down,
Give Mother Earth a chance to catch her breath—
Or go on doing what we do, while people drown
In coastal zones, and the planet faces death.

Sometimes when Appalachia's valleys brim
With clouds, her mountaintops appear to float
Like islands in a sea of white—a whim
Of nature in a landscape thought remote.

*Windmills are known to spew
Tremendous fumes and residue . . .*

Breaking Wind

The Donald never understood
That wind is clean, and pure, and good.
Although he's not a windmill fan,
He's studied them and therefore can
Declare with clear autonomy
How bad a wind economy
Would be. Windmills are known to spew
Tremendous fumes and residue,
A skill in which he's also versed.
He claims our tiny world is cursed—
A monster carbon footprint looms
If we continue spewing fumes
And "everything" into the air
That Germany and China share.
In keeping with his climate goal,
He'll stuff our stockings full of coal.

Oil Futures

Silt. Rifle. Parachute. Everywhere
along the Colorado River, between
the tank farms and the drilling rigs,
the sand-and-gravel strip mines and
the clustered dream homes dropped
on buttes and mesas, globe willows
and cottonwoods pose for photographs
showing how the river looked before
asphalt and plastic made scenery passé.

At the El Palomino Motel on North
Avenue in Grand Junction, chrome-
studded pick-up trucks with names
like Yukon, Avalanche and Silverado
surround the oval concrete island
where the placid swimming pool
reflects the setting sun. "Halliburton,"
beams the manager. "Full occupancy.
More workers rolling in every day."

After dark, a red *No Vacancy* blazes
beneath the white outline of a rearing
palomino on the motel sign, a relic
from the 1950s, before Interstate 70
bypassed the business district. Voices
hang in the heavy air. *¿Donde trabajaste?*
asks one. Where did you work? *Cantarell,*
comes the response. *Pero el petróleo se
está acabando.* But the oil is running out.

Downwinders

We see, reflected in the looking glass,
Old friends whose lives we seek to validate—
Reason enough to storm the gates en masse.

We grew up drinking milk from cows whose grass
Was tainted by atomic waste. The hate
We see reflected in the looking glass

Reminds us of the government's morass.
To hide their doubts and fears, they fabricate—
Reason enough to storm the gates en masse.

We die from cancer of the pancreas.
The government attributes this to fate.
We see, reflected in the looking glass,

Rebellion's fiery eyes. Forewarned of mass
Graves, we, the people, might repudiate
Reason—enough to storm the gates en masse.

We're told priorities are cast in brass.
They grease the war machine and cease debate.
We see, reflected in the looking glass,
Reason enough to storm the gates en masse.

The Dillowy Danderhonk

The Danderhonk in the Deacon's well
One day began to swell, and swell.
With no direction to go but up,
It rose and rose till the Deacon's cup
Ran over and all the townsfolk came
To wonder who in blank was to blame
For the dillowy Danderhonk.

In a blink it swallowed the Deacon's wife,
Who came at it waving a gravy knife,
Then the Deacon's dog and all he owned.
When it got his cat the Deacon groaned,
For gone was his little pride and joy,
The love of his life, his baby boy,
To the depths of the Danderhonk.

The beast spilled into a neighbor's yard
And turned the poor man's pigs to lard.
The townsfolk wrung their hands and prayed
As the Danderhonk advanced and made
A mockery of the dinkers they tossed,
Whose purpose, if one existed, was lost
In the flanks of the Danderhonk.

When the creature reached the edge of town,
The Grand Wyzee donned cap and gown
To pace up and down discussing the case
Of the Danderhonk's abuse of space.
Meanwhile the Deacon drowned his woes
At the Rub-a-Dub Pub to protect his nose
From the stink of the Danderhonk.

The townsfolk threw up their hands and fled
When the beast, by slow degrees, turned red
As the dimpled face of a cranberry bog
And spread like fleas on the Deacon's dog.
There was nothing anyone knew how to do
To stop the monster, and so it grew
To the dandiest Danderhonk.

Then a wisp of a miss came up and kissed
The Danderhonk and made it list,
And swoon, and shrink, and faint dead away,
And turn from a rosy hue to gray.
The beast, it appeared, had fed on fear,
And the girl, to be fair, shed a tiny tear
For the ghost of the Danderhonk.

To a Corrupt Politician

You stand stark naked in a light so hard
The warts rise from your skin in bold relief.
I stab you with stiletto eyes, bombard
Your blockhead with dumbfounded disbelief,
Upbraid your name with curses, cast your face
Among the demon hoards in dreams that seep
Up from the deep, dark muck. You lack the grace
To stand on principle, the slope too steep,
Yet dance for puppet masters who undrape
The landscape, penetrate past points where need
Or good is served beyond their own. If rape
Is violation, what on Earth is greed?
You stuff your hands in pockets lined with graft.
Am I along in seeing through your craft?

4
TRUMP: "WHAT I LOVE"

Apocalypse Now

The son of Pastor Billy Graham declared
That evangelicals believe the Prez,
An ordinary mortal unimpaired
By any virtue he thus far has shared,
Is Jesus Christ. Or so the Bible says.

In Franklin's eyes, the Prez is plagued with sin,
But aren't we all? So cut the guy some slack.
The Ten Commandments take it on the chin
But immorality is mostly spin
By humanists and others of their claque.

Some folks maintain that he's a total fraud
And takes His name in vain to fool the flock.
So why do fundamentalists applaud
And view him as the second Son of God?
Abortion rights. The rest is poppycock.

Bleating like a Billy goat,
Bloated as a fatted calf...

CNN Poll

Did or didn't Donald lie?
Nine percent give him the nod,
While ninety-one percent applaud
Old Glory, Mom, and Apple Pie,
The NSA, the FBI,
The NBA, the NFL, and God.

The nine percent say he will drain
The swamp, employ his business sense,
Fulfill his promise to dispense
With rules. Those with half a brain
Admit they're rich and hope to gain
A bigger share at no expense.

The ninety-one percent are split
On what it is they least admire
About a chief who likes to fire
Subordinates for counterfeit
Misdeeds, a flaming hypocrite
Who wallows in the muck and mire.

Some score his monumental lack
Of empathy and self-control,
Some shame his emphasis on coal
With solar, wind and wave on track
To blunt the CO_2 attack
As Earth grows warmer, pole to pole.

The vast majority would laugh
To see him lift aloft and float,
Bleating like a Billy goat,
Bloated as a fatted calf,
Out to sea, his epitaph:
"Putin had me by the throat."

Trump: "What I Love"

I love locking kids in cages,
Kissing up to rightwing thugs,
Laughing at starvation wages,
Pumping up the cost of drugs.

I love shutting down the poor,
Cutting taxes for the rich,
Acting like an utter boor,
Branding forceful women *Bitch!*

I love boasting Russian friends,
Bedding bimbos by the score,
Reaping Mitch's dividends,
Drumming up a global war.

I love watching cable news,
Taking cues from Hannity,
Hurling racist slurs at Jews,
Wallowing in vanity.

I love ogling shapely buns,
Handing jobs to nincompoops,
Shielding creeps who covet guns,
Praising neo-fascist groups.

I love preaching to the flock,
Forcing farmers on the dole,
Spouting lies and doubletalk,
Deepening the fiscal hole.

I love stiffing diplomats,
Blocking scans of tax returns,
Bashing leftwing Democrats,
Golfing while the planet burns.

Vlad The Impaler

If Vladimir has got the goods
On Donald, as we're hearing—
Those tête-à-têtes with Russian hoods,
That talk of racketeering,

Suspicious deals where real estate
Was used to launder money,
Entrapments dangling girls as bait—
Who wouldn't find it funny

That Donald sets his foes ablaze
With equal sound and fury,
While heaping Vladimir with praise?
Let's leave it to the jury.

So what if Donald rigged the vote
And danced as Russia pulled his strings?

The Ho-Humness of Donald's Misdeeds

When Bill and Monica were hot
The coverage was round the clock.
The Trump and Russia tryst is caught
Between a hard place and a rock.

The media have Donald's tweets
To analyze before they choose
Whatever else there is that meets
The current acid test for news.

Reporters work for billionaires,
Which puts a yoke around their necks.
There's little interest in affairs
That don't dish up some sizzling sex.

So what if Donald rigged the vote
And danced as Russia pulled his strings?
He's wearing Reagan's Teflon coat
And Putin's Kevlar underthings.

Presidential Kiss-off

Dear Vladimir, my bosom buddy Vlad,
The Faux News media have found me out.
I fear my situation's looking bad.
My re-election chances are in doubt.
I've danced when you have pulled my strings,
Turned allies into foes and foes to friends,
Stirred discontent at home, and other things.
Your rubles have paid handsome dividends.
I may request asylum—are you on?
Your faithful and devoted servant, Don

Dear Donald, Comrade Don as you prefer,
I take it you are seeking my support.
Your media are right—I must concur.
I'd like to help, but I'm a little short.
The world is being primed for Russian rule.
My oligarchs and I have work to do.
We'll find another dupe who'll play the fool.
Truth is, we have no further use for you.
No hair spray, dressed in orange—be of good cheer
In prison! *Dasvedaniya,* Vladimir

5

TWO BROTHERS WITH BUT ONE REGRET

Alone Among the Creatures

> *Much Madness is divinest Sense—*
> *To a discerning Eye—*
> *Much Sense—the starkest Madness—*
>
> —Emily Dickinson

I look for justice in a leaf,
For fairness in a blade of grass,
Compassion at the tips of ferns,
Acceptance in a flower. Alas—

I see these qualities alive
In every form of life but mine,
The one I must by fate embrace
As grape clings to withered vine.

I cannot trust my fellow man
To hold his own ideals on high.
The creatures truest to themselves
Move on four legs, or swim, or fly.

There is no law above the Prez.

L'État, C'est Trump

As Prexy 45 now says,
There is no law above the Prez.
King Donald, as he'll soon be known,
Can flop upon his golden throne
And rule the universe by tweet
While toadies kneel and kiss his feet.
Once Moscow Mitch has scratched his itch,
He'll strategize, without a glitch,
On possibilities for graft
And giving Democrats the shaft.

Two Brothers With But One Regret

    Conference on Population Studies
    Portland, Oregon, April 1962

1/ Washington Park Zoo

His eyes pearl clad, he pitched
from the top step, landed on my back,
there in the keepers walk
beside the lion cage. I saved his life.
He died the day John Kennedy
was shot, eluded all but the few
who read Page Seventeen.

2/ Reed College

His eyes cat quick,
he strolled the campus walk
with measured step. I listened
hard, struck his gait, hands
clasped behind, feet pointed wide.
He carried a message
of such sweeping consequence
few who even took time to try
could comprehend.

3/ Bonneville Dam

My senses tuned, I took them
touring round, answered bone-clean
questions, prided my tutored
knowledge of the state.
They talked of the world,
of people I knew by name,
and mankind's destiny.

"Do you mean, Brother,
there is no hope?" I watched
Aldous ask. In my rearview mirror,
Sir Julian sat with sad, sad eyes
and simply shook his head.

6

HE LOOKED SO HANDSOME IN HIS UNIFORM

He Looked So Handsome in His Uniform

He looked so handsome in his uniform,
The medals on his chest displayed with pride
Despite the ugly scars of Vietnam,

The pinpoint death rained down in Desert Storm,
Iraqi Freedom's dirty underside.
He looked so handsome in his uniform

When comrades in his honor guard crossed swords
The day his one true love became his bride.
Despite the ugly scars of Vietnam,

He stayed close to the sacred oath he'd sworn,
To serve his country well. His widow cried—
He looked so handsome in his uniform

Laid out for relatives and friends to mourn,
Unanswered questions as to why he died.
Despite the ugly scars of Vietnam,

He clung to his ideals—to keep from harm
The innocent, the gentle, the untried.
He looked so handsome in his uniform
Despite the ugly scars of Vietnam.

Ballade for the Gods of War

If pen, indeed, is mightier than sword,
Then why does chaos thrive, despite the spate
Of dovish prose, like some barbaric horde
Rampaging toward an ancient Roman gate?
If words have force enough to liberate
The soul, then why is intellect inclined
To turn oblivious and unrefined,
And bow when gods of conflict seek release?
What is this aberration of the mind?
The sane alternative to war is peace.

All politicians say they seek accord.
Beneath the rhetoric a candidate
Propounds lurk campaign contributions poured
By profiteers. Their agents infiltrate
With messages that serve to mitigate
The search for common ground. They work behind
the scenes, these deputies of death, aligned
With bureaucratic sycophants, to grease
The war machine and rob the people blind.
The sane alternative to war is peace.

How long will we allow the overlord
Whose weapons drain our wealth to confiscate
The ship and toss our values overboard?
Where in this picture is the fourth estate,
Whose purpose is to quicken the debate?
A billion words endorsing war, combined,
Keep ammunition requisitions signed.
Unchecked, defense contractors flock like geese
To see the House and Senate wined and dined.
The sane alternative to war is peace.

Investment tentacles are intertwined.
These captains of conceit, their craft designed
To calm the swells, like Orwell's thought police
Leave carnage in their wake, incarnadined.
The sane alternative to war is peace.

The War To End All Wars

> America's first World War I memorial, a replica of Stonehenge,
> was dedicated July 4, 1918, on a bluff above the Columbia River
> at Maryhill, Washington

The names of those who perished in The War
To End All Wars, the youth whose county bears
The proud name of the Klickitat of lore,
Adorn the pillars cast like stones. The pairs

Of dates raised from the bronze reliefs add proof:
Those things in life we prize we throw to chance,
Our loyalties misplaced, our airs aloof.
Their blood still stains the battlefields of France.

We called our brand of cannon fodder *Boys!*
And cheered them as they marched to join the ranks
Of unmarked graves on foreign soil, the noise
Ear-piercing as the shells rained down, the tanks

Whined on their flanks, machine-gun bullets ripped
Their flesh. They grew to men in nothing flat,
While those who stayed at home reposed, and nipped
Their cordials on their patios, and grew too fat

To know the sacrament of sacrifice.
Ask Edward Lindblad, Dewey Bromley, James
D. Duncan, Robert Venable, the price
They paid for glory. Dead at nineteen, names

On plaques. James Henry Allen, twenty-one.
Young Harry Gottfredson, at twenty-four,
Some poor hardscrabble family's sacred son
Until the Captain knocked upon their door.

The Age of Innocence died at Verdun
In 1916. We played dead, our views
Provincial, though we ran to see, first run,
The faux heroics staged for Pathé News.

*We stopped them at the Marne / We beat them on
The Aisne / We gave them Hell at Neuve Chappelle
And here we are, yes, here we are . . .*

Our Doughboys sailed away to whoops and cheers
Those glory days in 1917,
"The Stars and Stripes Forever" in their ears,
And "Over There." So spirited, so green,

Was Robert Graham, a Leap Day baby born
In '96, eleven days would pass
Before he headed home, his body torn
Beyond repair, mowed down like meadow grass.

We stopped them at the Marne / We beat them on
The Aisne / We gave them Hell at Neuve Chappelle /
And here we are, yes, here we are ... all gone.
The eyes spring tears, the heart tattoos farewell.

"We Stopped Them at the Marne," words
and music by Lieutenant Gitz Rice, from
Songs the Soldiers and Sailors Sing, 1918

With Armageddon Just Around the Bend

Is it enough to sit and watch the fir
Boughs dancing in the late October breeze
Before November's winds begin to stir,
Immersed in admiration for the trees?

Of myriad sins, the deadliest is pain
Inflicted on a whim. There follow these:
Attenuation of all things humane.
The many heads of greed. Hypocrisies.

With Armageddon just around the bend,
False prophets seize the day and waltz their way
Past rule of law. Who'll lift the lid? Who'll send
The caveat? Who'll right the disarray?

Is it enough to sit and watch the boughs
Dance into night as long as light allows?

7
DAWN OF THE ANTHROPOCENE

I'm Glad My Parents and My Brother Died

I'm glad my parents and my brother died
Believing life would go on much the same.
Before the world committed suicide,

No one thought twice about the rising tide,
The import of whole forests set aflame.
I'm glad my parents and my brother died

Before we knew what "megastorm" implied,
Or melting glaciers in the shrinking frame
Before the world committed suicide.

Our trusted leaders, bought and paid for, lied
Before they tried to redirect the blame.
I'm glad my parents and my brother died

When people still could look about with pride
And not be overwhelmed with shame—
Before the world committed suicide,

Before the system took us for a ride,
Before we knew they viewed us as fair game.
I'm glad my parents and my brother died
Before the world committed suicide.

The End of the World

Twelve thousand years ago when melting ice
Made chains of islands of Nevada peaks
Like Yucca Mountain, born of sudden thrusts
Deep in the Earth—the grabens and the horsts,
Your classic block-and-basin stuff—no words
Foretold catastrophe. Yet nothing speaks
So clearly of what's coming next as this
Co-mingling of reality and dream,
Six active faults exposed by recent quakes,
Old percolations trailing travertine,
A burning need to bury lethal waste
So industry can underpin the myth
That out-of-sight means tight security
And all is well from sea to shining sea.

"Some say the world will end in fire, some say
In ice," wrote Robert Frost, who favored fire.
If he had known how radiation burns
Inside a person's bones and turns the flesh
To mush, he might have swung his weight to ice,
Which he admitted would suffice. He saw
The end of Mother Earth as clean and nice,
Not tortured by the specter of a slow
Excruciating metamorphosis,
Extinctions piled ahead on either hand
As radiation works its fingers up
The food chain, link by link. He saw
The way it used to be when nature dealt
The cards—volcano's fire or glacier's ice.

The Geologic Periodic Chart
Reads like a catalog of instant change.
Each tiny line within an Age divides
Survivors from unlucky ones who say,
Like trilobites to ammonites, "So long."
Milankovitch was first to note the bob
And weave of Earth, and correlate the mix
Of fire and ice. His interglacial mode
Is all we've known since people first set sail

And charted fertile coastlines clear to where
They saw the southern continents drop off.
There have been mass extinctions in the past.
The Permian-Triassic springs to mind,
Cretaceous-Tertiary close behind.

Nevada's Yucca Mountain has appeal.
It's miles from anywhere a body knows.
It offers jobs to locals out of work.
It paves the county roads and pays the cops.
It lends bravado to the good ol' boys
Who populate the local bars and play
The nickel slots, eyes on the tourist trade.
This wisdom doesn't mention backing off,
Though questions left unanswered point the way.
What happens when relentless climate change
Pours unaccustomed wetness up the cracks
That liken Yucca Mountain to a sponge,
Once polar icecaps melt entirely away
And ocean levels rise three hundred feet?

As soon as Mother Earth cools down and lets
Green things emerge from under rocks, the bugs
Will stir. Insectivores, some new, some old,
Will pop up from their holes. The skies will fill
With birds. In time, most monuments of man
Will vanish, cracked like Anasazi bowls,
Some ground to dust beneath advancing ice,
Some turned to slag in magma's molten churn.
Let's say that one day wind and rain and cold
Expose a western mountain's hollow flank.
Let's say that sentient creatures have again
Evolved who stand in awe before a site
Viewed as a tomb from prehistoric times.
What if they can't decode the signs we left?

Comes the Renaissance

In a dark time, the eye begins to see.
—Theodore Roethke

It has been prophesied that we will die
Like feedlot cattle, pigs, and chickens, penned
So tightly we have scarcely room to breathe,
In bondage to indifferent overlords.

Like cows and pigs and chickens penned
With no hope of escape, we face our fate,
Accepting unresponsive overlords
As if we have no means of righting wrongs.

With no hope of escape, we rail at fate
For keeping us locked up, yet mope about,
Forgetting our success at fighting back
When pressed against the wall by autocrats

Who keep us tightly bound. It's all about
How much we bear before we cry "No more!"
When pressed against the wall by autocrats,
We throw our elbows out and shout "Enough!"

How far we're pushed before we bear no more
Depends on how the least among us fare.
We throw our elbows out and shout "Enough!"
When we see those we care about oppressed.

To equalize how those among us fare,
We first must turn the strongholds upside down,
Standing arm in arm with those oppressed,
And shake them hard until the despots fall—

Though once we turn their strongholds upside down
And speed our callous masters to their doom,
We must resist the urge to shake so hard
That values we hold dear fall by the way.

Sending despots tumbling to their doom
Presages what comes next, a renaissance
That builds upon the values we hold dear,
As brilliant in their phases as the dawn.

A taste of what's to come—the renaissance
Foreseen by prophets of a rising faith
As dazzling as a rainbow arc at dawn—
Shows people joining hands to set a course

Foretold by oracles who warned we'll die
If we stay penned by oligarchs, like sheep,
So tightly we have scarcely room to breathe.
In these dark times, the eye begins to see.

I Dream of Bells

I dream the world is wobbling like a top,
No longer doing what it's always done.
Rough voices raised in anger scattergun
Atrocities they're powerless to stop.
Fierce windstorms slaughter animal and crop
Bombarded by unfiltered bursts of sun.
Silksuited moguls scrap their gold and run
From frenzied mobs until the last ones drop.
I wake beneath an opalescent sky,
Flat on my back on some abandoned beach.
The sandstone cliffs are lined with empty shells
Of cottages. Some distance off, the cry
Of seagulls seeking something out of reach,
The pounding surf, the pealing steeple bells.

On the Rebirth of America

The new millennium is underway
At last, held hostage for a raft of years
By home-grown architects of disarray,
Sly profiteers who played upon our fears
Like harpists plucking strings. They made us dance
Two-step when all we wanted was to waltz
Through life with satisfying jobs, good health,
The basics—justice, truth. Imagine, France
Held up to ridicule for branding false
A bald-faced lie! So much for rule by stealth.

The founders of this nation knew the time
Would come when we'd be forced to reassess
Core values, reach past artful to sublime,
Endure the pain accompanying redress.
Supremely optimistic, they left clues
To solve the riddles of this lawless age.
Found in their writings are the truths we hold
To be self-evident. Now we must choose
Between two futures, one defying sage
Advice, the other confident and bold.

Beginning now, let's paint the future bright.
It may take years to put us on the path
To universal health care and the right
To pick lifestyles that fit, without the wrath
Of righteous indignation crashing down—
But here we are, survivors of the best
The enemy within could muster, free
Of ringmaster and charismatic clown,
The beasts who fed upon our wealth. The test
Will be to redefine democracy.

Dawn of the Anthropocene

No matter what we know about the past,
We haven't got a clue to what's in store
Tomorrow, just that it's approaching fast.

Some people place their faith in ancient lore,
Believing everything on Earth is wrapped
Up in one package and there's nothing more

To do but wait—which is to say, we're trapped
In transcendental limbo-land, our fate
Ordained, as if it's pointless to adapt

To changing circumstances: It's too late
To save the planet from the end-time scourge
So dive into the pool and pick a date.

Some people entertain a frantic urge.
Hot blood courses through their hardened veins.
They know to let go of the reins and splurge

On all the luxuries ill-gotten gains
Can buy, remote enclaves, their cellars stocked
With wine enough to ride the tide, domains

Protected by thick walls, their weapons cocked
Against the vengeances of blackened air,
Their shuttered doors and windows triple-locked.

Other people quietly prepare
To do what's necessary to survive,
Immerse themselves, make certain they're aware

Of everything they'll need to stay alive.
These are the ones whose lines will clear the stage
For players in the Anthropocene, who'll thrive

As mammals did when a meteor turned the page
On dinosaurs. As Shakespeare wrote, *What's past
Is prologue.* Greet the new communal age.

Tomorrow

The green snake with the white stripe coils like a hose,
The sentinel stands like an old milk can ripe with rust,
The dancers show frilly gold underpants like dandelions
Bent against a gust, the lacy lady blazes bright green trails
Across the broad lawn like a maple tree in April breeze.

I sit in the window sipping at a cup, drinking the draft
Of a scene that reels like tipsy ballerinas in a chorus
From a *danse profane,* making love with the tip of my nose
Against the steamy pane to all I see, breathing a breath
Deeper than the whole of space, headier than any sneeze.

I was naïve in an age where innocence played like a game,
Innocent beyond the frame of my peers' imaginings, a tool
Of the bright sides of left and right, a fool juggling oranges
With bare feet, an acolyte of truth and beauty seeking balance
In a world of false beliefs, a permanent thaw in the freeze.

The game changes daily, and the innocent are swept to sea
Like flotsam on the swollen crests of rivers gone aflood,
Bobbing in their tiny private worlds of no return, unseen
By all the eyes turned inward on their dreams, the souls
Bent only on the goal of only doing only what they please.

I was a child when I awoke today, gazing out with wonder
On a world of lustrous color, pretty, luminous, and bright,
And up my sleeve I carried mischief like the magic coins
My Uncle Hank popped from my ears, his long thin fingers
Nimble as spiders' legs, eyes swimming in tiny salty seas.

I will see with a child's eyes until the day I die, and I
Would have that day be mellow as a bumblebee afloat on air
Thick with the scents of daphne odora, lilac, and narcissus,
Abloom with all the splendor they muster, or hummingbirds
Flitting among the sweet juicy blossoms of catalpa trees.

I would have that day alive with cries of children innocent
Beyond their needs, freedom's arms wrapped tight in a hug
Snug as a bug in a rug, innocent as all get out, like music
In a park on a picnic blanket under summer skies, what
My Uncle Hank would laugh and call "the bee's knees."

I would have tomorrow be that way if I could wave a wand
And tack humanity far from harm, or simply chart a bearing
Somewhere off away, apart from where tomorrow seems about
To turn the world topsy-turvy, where everyone gets together
And in one way or another, somehow, to some extent, agrees.

Tomorrow I will learn why the songs in my heart sometimes
Stray off-key, why the baling wire and chewing gum I use
To hold my sagging parts in place may need to be exchanged
For what my Uncle Hank would turn thumbs-down on, "fancy
Doodads," and why I find my life caught in a real squeeze.

Today I am immersed in sunlight, the green of maple leaves
Wavering between light and shadow, the canopy I sit beneath
Billowing in a sudden gust and settling, with delicate sigh
And solemnity, to points where branches hang in the balance,
Poised breathless for the crush of unexpected eventualities.

ABOUT THE AUTHOR

Poet and author David Hedges has a long history of political involvement. He served as an aide to two majority leaders in the  Oregon House of Representatives, as well as to Multnomah County and Portland City commissioners. He worked as a paid professional on more than 60 political campaigns at state and local levels, including a governor's race in Alaska, and was state coordinator for a presidential campaign. He was dubbed an "environmental warrior" by the Oregon League of Conservation Voters for saving Canemah Bluff, once home to as many as 60,000 Indigenous people during seasonal salmon runs at the Falls of the Willamette, from a housing development. His first book, *Petty Frogs on the Potomac* (1997), pokes fun, in rhymed verse, at Newt Gingrich's 1994 Republican Revolution, and Bill Clinton's wavering response. He lives in Oregon City, where his Oregon Trail ancestors settled in the mid-1800s. View his work at david.hedges.name.

ABOUT THE ARTIST

Illustrator Jim Agpalza lives outside Portland, Oregon, where he pursues his career as a freelance illustrator, cover artist, character designer, and storyboard artist. His work has appeared in numerous formats, including cartoons, books, comics, slot machines, and T-shirts. He is co-creator and character designer for the animated show *Spacefish,* the novel *Fantastic Earth Destroyer Ultra Plus,* and the comic book, *Crusader of Sin.* He has illustrated works by many authors, including Theodore Sturgeon and Isaac Isamov, and book covers for such acclaimed authors as Shane McKenzie and Edward Lee, and for Eraserhead Press, Deadite Press, and Lazy Fascist. In 2022, he created the cover for *Trump Über Alles: Rhymes for Trying Times,* a chronicle, in light verse, of the former president's term in office, authored by David Hedges and published by Road's End Press. View examples of his artwork at jimagpalza.com.

www.ingramcontent.com/pod-product-compliance
Lightning Source LLC
Chambersburg PA
CBHW042353070526
44585CB00028B/2918